MW00748838

4942543

The **Muslim** Experience

Jan Thompson

Foundation

Hodder & Stoughton

A MEMBER OF THE HODDER HEADLINE GROUP

Acknowledgements

Dedicated to:
Lynne Broadbent, a friend and colleague

> *Notes:*
> Whenever Muslims speak or write Muhammad's name, they usually add 'Peace be upon him'. (Sometimes written as 'pbuh'.) It is a sign of respect. This book does not follow this practice because this is a text book for the general school population. This is not intended to be disrespectful. When Muslim pupils read aloud from this book they may wish to add these words wherever the Prophet's name occurs.
>
> CE = Common Era
> BCE = Before the Common Era
>
> CE corresponds to AD, and BCE corresponds to BC. The years are the same, but CE and BCE can be used by anyone regardless of their religion. (AD and BC are Christian: AD stands for Anno Domini – in the Year of Our Lord, i.e. Jesus Christ; BC stands for Before Christ.)

Orders: please contact Bookpoint Ltd, 39 Milton Park, Abingdon, Oxon OX14 4TD. Telephone: (44) 01235 400414, Fax: (44) 01235 400454. Lines are open from 9.00–6.00, Monday to Saturday, with a 24 hour message answering service. Email address: orders@bookpoint.co.uk

British Library Cataloguing in Publication Data
A catalogue record for this title is available from The British Library

ISBN 0 340 77582 3

First published 2000
Impression number   10 9 8 7 6 5 4 3 2 1
Year   2005 2004 2003 2002 2001 2000

Copyright © 2000 Jan Thompson, JF Aylett and Kevin O'Donnell

All rights reserved. No part of this publication may be produced or transmitted in any form or by any means, electronic or mechanical, including photocopy, recording, or any information storage and retrieval system, without permission in writing from the publisher or under licence from the Copyright Licensing Agency Limited. Further details of such licences (for reprographic reproduction) may be obtained from the Copyright Licensing Agency Limited, of 90 Tottenham Court Road, London W1P 9HE.

Cover photo from CIRCA, Photo Library
All illustrations supplied by Daedalus with special thanks to John McIntyre and Mohamed Abu Mustapha.
Typeset by Wearset, Boldon, Tyne and Wear.
Printed for Hodder & Stoughton Educational, a division of Hodder Headline Plc, 338 Euston Road, London NW1 3BH by Printer Trento, Italy

Key words are explained in the glossary on page 63.

The publishers would like to thank the following for permission to reproduce material in this book:

BBC Radio for the extract from *Quest*; BBC Television for the extract from *Third Eye*; Channel Four Television Company Ltd for the extracts from *Muslims in Britain*, a Priory Production for Channel 4 Television Company Ltd; Christian Education Movement for the extract from *RE Today*; The Muslim Educational Trust for the extracts from *The 4th Revised Edition of Islam Beliefs and Teachings* (1989); Time Life Books Inc for the extract from *Great Ages of Man: Early Islam* by Desmond Stewart and the Editors of Time Life Books, © 1967 Time Life Books Inc.; TVS Production Ltd for the extract from the *Human Factor* programme (1988); Unwin Hyman Ltd for the extract from *Rugs to Riches* by Caroline Bosley (1981).

Minor adaptations have been made to some quotations to render them more accessible to the readership.

The authors and publishers thank the following for permission to reproduce copyright photographs in this book:

Associated Press AP: pp7r, 59; Mark Azavedo: p47; La Bibliotheque Nationale: p10; Circa Photo Library: pp4, 6t, 58r (William Holtby), 19l, 19br (Barrie Searle), 43, 55 (John Smith), 6b, 31, 54r; Corbis: p42; Edward Arnold: p12; Sonia Halliday Photographs: p16, 24l; Life File: p27l (Dave Thompson); Christine Osborne/MEP: pp11, 40 (Camerapix), 21, 23, 24r, 30, 33, 34, 35, 37, 39, 41, 44, 45, 46, 50, 51, 52, 53, 54l, 57, 58l, 60, 62; David Rose: pp7l, 8, 19tr, 27r, 32, 49; Jan Thompson: p17; Topkapi Museum: p22; Travel Ink: p48 (Joanna Wilsher).

Every effort has been made to contact the holders of copyright material but if any have been inadvertently overlooked, the publishers will be pleased to make the necessary alterations at the first opportunity.

Contents

3

◄ *Islam is a world-wide religion*

4

Muslims can be from any country or race. Their religion is called Islam.

Find the letters 's','l' and 'm' in the words 'Muslim' and 'Islam'. In Arabic 'slm' means 'peace' or 'obey'. So 'Islam' means a 'the way of peace' and a Muslim is someone who obeys God.

Muslims call God 'Allah'. Islam teaches that a person finds peace in this life by obeying Allah. The very first chapter of the Muslim holy book talks about obeying Allah:

> In the name of Allah, the Merciful, the Compassionate …
> You alone we worship, and to You alone we pray for help.
> Help us to follow the right path.

Again, their holy book, the Qur'an says:

> It was He who sent down peace into the hearts of the faithful …
>
> *Qur'an 48 verse 4*

We have many choices in life. If you are selfish you can hurt other people as well as yourself. Muslims would say that it hurts God, too.

▲ *We can choose to follow different paths in life*

We choose how to behave. Many times in everyday life we have to choose right or wrong paths.

Muslims believe that Allah helps them to follow the right path. This gives them peace of mind.

● What would you do?

- John has been given an expensive CD player for his birthday. He brings it to school.
- Michael would really like one, too. But there is no way he can afford it.
- Paula wants to buy some new clothes. She decides to steal the CD player and sell it to Michael for whatever he will give her. She will be happy to get £20 for it.

Paula sees her chance in the PE lesson. She takes the CD from the teacher's office and passes it out of the window to Rachel. Rachel is on a cross-country run. She hides it in some bushes.

At the end of the lesson, John asks for his CD player. There is panic when it can't be found, and everyone is searched. The headteacher is told. John phones home and his father tells the police, but the school doesn't know this.

Paula offers the CD player to Michael. He is very tempted. This is his only chance to have one.

In groups, choose one or other of these role-plays. In one, Michael buys the CD player. In the other, he refuses. Think about their feelings, and what might happen next.

1 Islam teaches that it is wrong to steal. List FIVE things that you think are wrong.

2 In pairs, think up another situation where young people have to choose between a right or wrong path.

"As-Islām"

▲ *ISLAM written in beautiful Arabic*

The language of Islam is Arabic. It is often written in beautiful artwork.

▲ *A Muslim mosque*

A Muslim place of worship is called a mosque. Mosques usually have a dome and a tall tower.

▲ *A prayer mat*

Muslims use prayer mats so that they pray in a clean place. They face towards Makkah in Arabia when they pray.

The symbol of Islam is a moon and 5-pointed star. It doesn't matter which way it faces.

Key words
Arabic
mosque

6

Many people in the West have a bad view of Muslims. The news often shows them using violence in the name of God. Most Muslims are not like this. They live peaceful lives.

In the same way, people would have a strange view of Christianity if they only ever saw pictures of the bombings in Northern Ireland.

▲ *A Western terrorist*

The Muslim name for God is Allah. This is Arabic for 'the God'. Muslims believe in 'the one God'. This is the same God as Jews and Christians worship.

▲ *A Muslim commits him or herself to God and prays for peace*

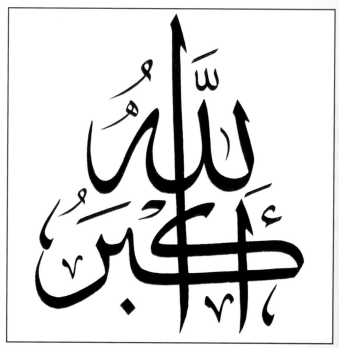

▲ *This says in Arabic 'Allah is the Greatest'*

1 Put the title over 2 columns: Introducing Muslims.
   a) Draw the symbol of Islam.
   b) Match up the following:

Islam means	the Qur'an
Followers of Islam are called	Arabic
The language of Islam is	peace
Their holy book is called	Muslims

◄ *Some things in life take your breath away*

Nature is so wonderful! Have you seen a tiny baby bird? Have you ever seen an animal being born? Have you stood beneath a starry sky? Have you been awake at dawn? Have you heard the power of a waterfall? Have you looked down on the clouds from an aeroplane?

Read how this American woman felt in the USA:

> I felt great joy. I knew that if this beauty was in everything around me, then it must also be within me. My heart broke open. My soul leapt free.

This opened her up to start believing in God. We can't prove that God exists. It is a matter of faith. Faith is often felt in the heart:

> God can only be felt inside. God cannot be measured with a ruler, or proved by maths. It is not that simple.

Muslims believe that God made the universe. The wonder of nature all around them tells them that God exists. They believe that all life comes from God. They bow before him and offer him praise for the wonderful world he has made.

● The One and Only

Most religions today teach that there is only one God. But this has not always been the case. Long ago, people believed in many gods. They worshipped the Sun-god, and the Moon-god. They worshipped the gods of the wind, fire, and water. As time went by, ideas changed. This was usually because of the message of prophets. A prophet is someone who speaks for God. One such prophet was Muhammad. He taught the people of Arabia that there was only one supreme God. They must worship him alone.

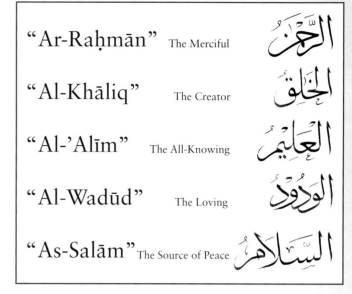

"Ar-Raḥmān" The Merciful

"Al-Khāliq" The Creator

"Al-'Alīm" The All-Knowing

"Al-Wadūd" The Loving

"As-Salām" The Source of Peace

▲ *Some of the 'Beautiful Names' in Arabic*

▲ *Islam teaches that people should love God with all their hearts*

Muslims say these names in their prayers. They have prayer-beads with 99 beads to help them. These names teach them what God is like.

There are no images of God in Islam. It teaches that God is so great that humans can never picture him in their minds, or make statues of him. He is unseen.

The Qur'an is the Muslim holy book. It has 99 'Beautiful Names' for God:

▲ *Some of the 'Beautiful Names' in English*

1 Try this exercise. Sit still and be quiet. Imagine you are walking in a beautiful wood. You stop to listen to the sounds. A branch snaps. A bird flies. Some leaves move. What else do you see and hear. After the exercise, list all the sights and sounds. Describe how it made you feel.

2 Think about times when you might feel the wonder of nature.

3 In pairs, choose ONE of the 'Beautiful Names'. Talk about what it means. Write it down and decorate it. Suggest what it teaches Muslims about God.

A Man called Muhammad

About the year 570 CE (**Common Era**), a baby boy was born in Makkah in what is now Saudi Arabia. He was called **Muhammad.**

His father died just a few weeks before he was born. When he was 6, his mother died also. He was brought up at first by his grandfather, and then his uncle.

A legend says that a Christian monk met the boy. He was very impressed by him. He said that he would become a prophet. (A prophet is someone who speaks for God.)

As a boy, Muhammad looked after sheep.

When he grew up he was proud of his work. He said, 'Allah sent no prophet who was not a shepherd.'

Muhammad became a trader. He travelled across the desert with his goods. He was honest and hard-working.

He was spotted by a rich woman called Khadijah. She asked him to look after her business. On his first trip to Syria, he made twice the money that she had expected! Soon after this, she asked him to marry her, although she was 40 and he was only 25. They married and were very happy together.

10

Key words
prophet **Makkah** **Ka'bah** **Khadijah**

▶ *This old picture shows a Muslim trader setting off on a journey*

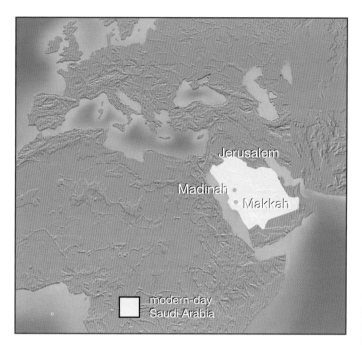

▲ *Muhammad's homeland is now called Saudi Arabia*

Makkah was a religious centre before Muhammad made it the centre of Islam. There was a special building there called the Ka'bah. (This means cube. It describes the shape of the building.) In its wall was a special black stone. It was said to have come from heaven. It is probably a meteorite.

One year the Ka'bah had been repaired and the stone had to be put back. Then the arguments started. Each tribe wanted the honour of doing it. In the end, an old man had an idea. The first person to walk through the temple gates next day would be asked to sort it out.

That person turned out to be Muhammad. He had the answer. They put the stone in a cloak and each tribe took a corner. In this way, they all carried it to the Ka'bah. Then Muhammad put it in place.

This is an early description of Muhammad: Handsome, medium height, thick black hair and beard, wide forehead, heavy eyebrows, large dark eyes below long lashes, wide chest and shoulders.

▲ *The Ka'bah in Makkah*

1 a) Write down any words from this list which you think describe a good shepherd: kind, watchful, lazy, calm, patient, bad-tempered, caring.
b) Which of these qualities are also useful for dealing with people?

2 Read the story about the black stone.
a) Why was Muhammad's answer clever?
b) Why do you think the people didn't mind him putting the stone in its place?
c) Can you think of a time when someone has solved a problem for you?

◄ *Cave Hira on the Mount of Light*

Now that Muhammad was married to Khadijah, he was a rich man. He could spend more time in prayer. Each year, during the month of Ramadan, he went alone to a cave called Hira, outside the city. The fifth year that he did this, he had a surprise visitor!

One night, an angel came to Muhammad and told him to read. But Muhammad had never learnt to read and write. Three times Muhammad told the angel that he could not read. Three times the angel squeezed him hard. Then the angel taught Muhammad this verse:

> Read: In the name of your Lord.
> Who made man from a clot of blood.
> Read: Your Lord is most Generous.
> Who taught by the pen.
> Taught man what he did not know.
> *Qur'an 96 verses 1–5*

This was the first of many meetings with the angel. At first Muhammad was afraid. He thought he was going mad. But the people who knew him best believed him.

A Christian told him that the angel was Gabriel. **Muhammad came to believe that God was calling him to be his prophet.**

> O Khadijah, the time for sleep and rest is past. Gabriel has asked me to warn men and call them to Allah and to His worship.

So Muhammad began to tell people that there was only one God. They must stop worshipping stone idols. They must lead good lives.

At first, only his close friends and relatives believed what he said. But he carried on preaching. He believed that God had given him this message.

Key words

Muhammad
angel
Gabriel
Ramadan
Madinah
Hijrah

12

◀ *This green dome is built over Muhammad's tomb. It is at a mosque in Madinah*

Muhammad's message was not welcome in Makkah. Many people travelled there to worship the idols. People in Makkah made a living from religion. They did not want Muhammad to ruin this. So they said he was a liar and they beat up his followers.

One day, visitors from the city of Yathrib heard Muhammad preach. They asked him to come and live there. It was over 300 kilometres away, across the desert.

Life became very dangerous for Muhammad. His enemies plotted to kill him. So, in the year 622 CE, Muhammad left Makkah to go to Yathrib. This city was to become famous because Muhammad lived there for the rest of his life. It became known as the town of the Prophet – or just Madinah (the Arabic for 'town').

This move from Makkah to Madinah is a very important event for Muslims. It is called the Hijrah. The Muslim calendar starts from this point. So AD 622 was AH 1 (in the first year of the Hijrah).

The legend of the spider's web

There is a legend that the enemies of Muhammad followed him from Makkah. Muhammad hid in a cave. A spider spun its web across the entrance. His enemies saw the web and thought that he could not have gone into the cave. So they moved on and Muhammad was safe.

1 Have *you* ever been criticised or attacked because you stuck up for what was right? Tell the rest of the class about it.

2 Finish off these sentences to explain what you have learned in this chapter:
- In Cave Hira, Muhammad met _____.
- In Makkah, Muhammad taught_____.
- When he was attacked, Muhammad left_____.

▲ *Each of us is special*

- Each person is special, one of a kind. Each of us has about 100,000 genes, which determine all sorts of things about us, like how we look.
- The way our bodies work is amazing. Our eyes can see more than the largest telescope. Our lungs could be spread out to cover a tennis court. When we touch something, we send messages to our brain at 124 mph.
- Our bodies form a living person with thoughts and feelings. We each have our own personality. No matter how much we take after other people, we are still different.

Muhammad wanted the Arabs to remember who made them. He wanted them to respect human life. The Arab tribes at that time often fought each other. Young men were killed in battle. This is why men were allowed to have many wives. There were more women than men. The widows and orphans had to be cared for. It is also the reason why baby girls were often killed at birth. There were too many women to look after. Muhammad did not allow such things in Islam. Islam teaches that everyone is special because God made them.

1 Make a poster about yourself, saying 'I'm special' or 'I'm unique.' Include on it photos of yourself, things to do with your hobbies, favourite music, etc.

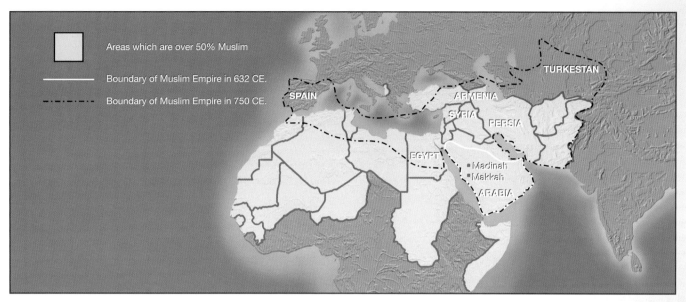

▲ *How the Muslim Empire grew in the 100 years after Muhammad's death. The key shows how Islam is still the main religion in these areas today*

Fighting went on between Makkah and Madinah for some years. Muhammad was a great soldier and leader. Finally, he conquered Makkah in 630 CE. Muhammad spared his enemies, but destroyed all the idols in the Ka'bah. The Ka'bah is still an empty building to this day. It is the centre of Islam. It shows that God is too great to have images made of him.

By the time of his death in 632, Muhammad had united most of Arabia under Islam. His good friend, Abu Bakr became leader after him. He too was a great leader. He was able to hold the Muslims together. He was also a humble man. He told the people:

> I have been chosen by you as your leader, but I am no better than any one of you. If I do any good, support me. If I do wrong, set me right. . . Obey me as long as I obey Allah and his messenger.

The main spread of Islam took place in the 100 years after Muhammad's death. It gradually spread north to Syria, further into Persia (now called Iran) and beyond into Turkestan (now called Afghanistan). Find these countries on the map above.

It spread west into Egypt, and further along the northern part of Africa. At one point the Muslim armies crossed the Mediterranean Sea into Spain. In 732, exactly a century after Muhammad died, Islam reached its furthest point west. The Muslim armies had marched through Spain into France. Here they were defeated at the town of Tours.

Muslims wanted to spread their religion because they believed that it was the right religion for everyone, not just the Arabs. However, the Qur'an makes it clear that they should not force people to become Muslims. Christians and Jews were often happy to be ruled by Muslims. They all worship the same God.

The Qur'an teaches that Muslims should not fight unless it is in self defence.

'People who are attacked can fight back. . .'   *Qur'an 22 verse 39*

'God does not love people who start a fight'   *Qur'an 2 verse 187*

The early Muslim armies fought back when rulers tried to stop people worshipping as Muslims. They defended their rights and their lands. This led to the birth of a great Muslim empire.

This empire split up in the 13th century. But Islam itself went on spreading. In Africa, Muslim traders went south. They took their religion with them. Towns were set up down the east coast of Africa 500 years before the Portuguese explorers got there. Traders also took Islam across the Indian Ocean to the Far East.

Damascus, the capital of Syria, was captured soon after Muhammad's death. This is what the Arab commander, Khalid, said:

> In the name of Allah, the Merciful, the Compassionate. This is what Khalid ibn al-Walid would grant to the people of Damascus . . . He promises to give them safety for their lives, property and churches. Their city wall shall not be knocked down . . . So long as they pay the tax, nothing but good shall befall them.

▼ *These Muslim travellers are being welcomed as they pass through a Syrian town in the 13th century*

1 The message of Islam spread far and wide. If you were given ONE minute on TV to give ONE message to the world, what would you say?

2 Talk with a partner about how Khalid treated the people of Damascus. What FIVE things did he promise them? Why do you think he treated them like this? Look at page 15 and find a reason why he didn't force them to become Muslims?

Muslims respect Jesus Christ as a great prophet. A prophet is someone who speaks for God. Muslims believe that God has sent prophets down through the ages, to bring people his messages. They believe that Adam was the first prophet and that Muhammad was the last. Many of their prophets can also be found in the Bible. Look at this list below:

Adam
Enoch
Noah
Abraham
Ishmael
Isaac
Lot
Jacob
Joseph
Job
Moses
Aaron
Ezekiel
David
Solomon
Elias/Elijah
Elisha
Jonah
Zechariah
John (the Baptist)
Jesus

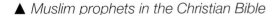

▲ *Muslim prophets in the Christian Bible*

In the Qur'an, Jesus is called Isa ibn Mariam al Masih. This is Arabic for 'Jesus, son of Mary, the Messiah'.

▲ *An old painting of Jesus*

Muslims believe that Jesus was the prophet before Muhammad. He is therefore given special respect. Muslims believe that he was a perfect human being who was born from a virgin. The Qur'an says that Jesus healed people by miracles. He is also called Messiah – God's chosen one (Christians believe these things too.) In the Qur'an, Jesus says:

'I am the servant of Allah. He has given me the Gospel and made me a prophet. His blessing is upon me wherever I go.'

Christians believe that Jesus was God living as a man. Muslims do not agree that Jesus was God. Muhammad made it clear to Muslims that he too was only a man. He was afraid that they might worship him, as Christians worship Jesus. He once said:

'Do not praise me as the Christians have praised Jesus. I am only God's servant. Call me the servant and messenger of God.'

Unlike Christians, most Muslims believe that Jesus was too holy to die on the cross. They believe another man died in his place. Or a trick was played on the crowd, and he was taken up to heaven to be with God.

However, like Christians, all Muslims believe that Jesus will return before the final Day of Judgement. Muhammad said:

'I swear by Him who holds my life between His hands, Jesus will come back down among you very soon as a fair judge.'

He once spoke of a vision he had had:

> Then I noticed a brown-skinned man with smooth hair which was wet. Water was dripping from it onto the ground. I asked who it was. I was told, 'It's Jesus.'

Christians call Jesus 'the Son of God'. Muslims disagree because the Qur'an teaches that Allah has no son.

However, the Qur'an describes Jesus as 'a word sent from Allah'. Christians also call Jesus the 'Word of God'.

There are differences between Muslims and Christians about Jesus. But many try to respect each other's beliefs as they share and talk together.

◄ *A picture of the vision of Jesus that Muhammad saw. Is it likely that Jesus looked like this?*

1 Make a list from pages 17–18 of NINE things the Qur'an says about Jesus.

2 a) In what ways do Muslims differ from Christians in their beliefs about Jesus?
b) What do they believe about Jesus which is the same as Christians?

▲ Jewish Western Wall

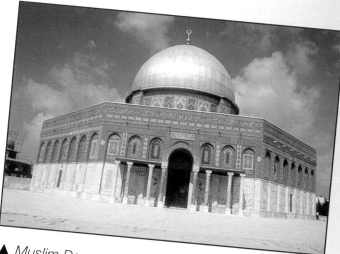

▲ Muslim Dome of the Rock

Jerusalem is a holy city to Jews, Muslims and Christians. The photos on this page show:

- the Western Wall – this wall holds up the mound where the Jewish temple once stood. It is all that is left of the temple site.
- the Dome of the Rock – this early mosque was built over a large rock. This is where Muslims believe Muhammad went up to heaven. They believe that he returned with teachings about Muslim prayer.
- the Church of the Holy Sepulchre – this church was built over the place where Christians believe Jesus was buried.

At first, Muhammad and the Muslims faced towards Jerusalem when they prayed (just as Jews do), but later he changed this. Muslims now face towards the Ka'bah in Makkah when they pray. Although the Ka'bah had been used for idols, Muslims believe that it was the very first mosque. They believe it was built by Adam, and later rebuilt by Abraham.

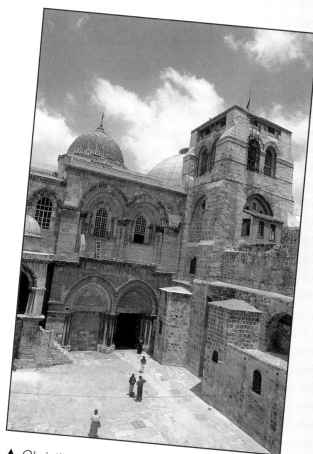

▲ Christian Church of the Holy Sepulchre

The 3 religions have fought each other over who controls Jerusalem. Much blood has been shed. There are still arguments over who owns the land in this area.

Christians and Muslims fought each other in the Crusades of the Middle Ages. These were wars in the Holy Land. Christians fought to win back the lands that the Muslims ruled there. They wore red crosses on their tunics to show that they fought for Christ.

Sometimes the Muslim rulers were fair to Jews and Christians. They showed respect for their holy places. This is shown in a story about the early Muslim ruler, Omar. When he captured Jerusalem in 638 CE, he was taken around the holy city. He was in the Church of the Holy Sepulchre, when it was time for the Muslim prayers. Omar wouldn't pray in the church itself, but he went outside. He knew that if he prayed inside the church, his followers would claim it for Islam. So this church was left in the hands of the Christians.

How different was the story of the first Crusade. When the Christians captured Jerusalem in 1099, they killed all the Muslims and Jews in the city.

The most famous crusader to capture Jerusalem was Richard I of England. He was so brave that he was called Richard the Lionheart. The Muslim leader at the time was Saladin. He too was a very brave soldier and leader. The two men had great respect for each other. Saladin even sent a box of snow and fresh fruit to the king when he was ill with fever.

Saladin showed mercy to his enemies. But Richard could be very cruel. When he captured the town of Acre, he had thousands of Muslims killed. He was afraid that they would rejoin Saladin and fight against him.

At the end of the 20th century, Pope John Paul II apologised for the Crusades. He spoke for the Roman Catholic Church. Other Christians took part in a special walk. They walked to all the places where the crusaders had been. They went there to pray and ask God to forgive the Church for the terrible things that it did all those years ago.

▲ *A drawing of Richard and Saladin, whose helmet falls off to show his devil's face. Christian drawings at the time showed the enemy as evil and cruel*

1 Why did Christians fight and kill Muslims in the Crusades?

2 a) Do you think 2 people with different views can still be friends?
b) Think of 2 different groups of people who don't get on today. What do you think the Pope would say to them?

3 a) Why do you think Christians went to the Holy Land to say sorry for the Crusades?
b) Have you ever made a special effort to say sorry?

◄ Muslims say the 'Bismillah' before going on a journey

Before Muslims eat their food, or go on a journey, they say a quiet prayer to themselves (ask your teacher to read it):

Bismillah-ir-Rahman-ir-Rahim.

This means '**In the name of God, the Merciful, the Compassionate**'.

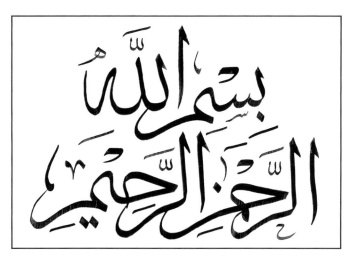

▲ The 'Bismillah' in Arabic

These are the first words of the Qur'an, the Muslim holy book. And they are the first words of nearly every chapter of the Qur'an. To a Muslim, it is a holy phrase. It sums up a lot about God.

The 'Bismillah' is in Arabic. This is the language of Islam. It is the language that Muhammad spoke because he lived in Arabia. The Muslim holy book is written in Arabic. Muslims believe that it will lose some of its meaning if it is changed into other languages. So Muslims who do not speak Arabic have to learn it. There are special classes at the mosque to teach children to read the Qur'an in Arabic.

> And He (God) commands you, saying: This is my straight path, so follow it. Do not follow other paths.
>
> *Qur'an 6 verse 153*

Muslims believe that the Qur'an is exactly as it was told to Muhammad. It was not given all at once, but in parts over 23 years.

As Muhammad could not write, he chose people to write it down. Few Arabs could read and write in those days. But they had a gift for learning things by heart. Today, all Muslims learn parts of the Qur'an by heart. They begin with the 'Bismillah' which they try to learn by their 4th birthday. Some people can recite the whole of the Qur'an. The Qur'an has about 78,000 words. (This book has about 15,000.)

Muhammad died in 632 and many Muslims were killed in battle. Abu Bakr, who became leader after Muhammad, worried that the words of God would be lost. So the Qur'an was written in one book. It was checked by those who had heard it from Muhammad. This copy was made less than 2 years after Muhammad died. All modern copies of the Qur'an are the same as this.

Muslims believe that the Qur'an contains the words of God, and not the words of Muhammad. Muhammad's own teachings are written in books called the Hadith. Muslims like to follow his example. They can find in these books what Muhammad said and did.

Key words

Bismillah
Qur'an
Hadith

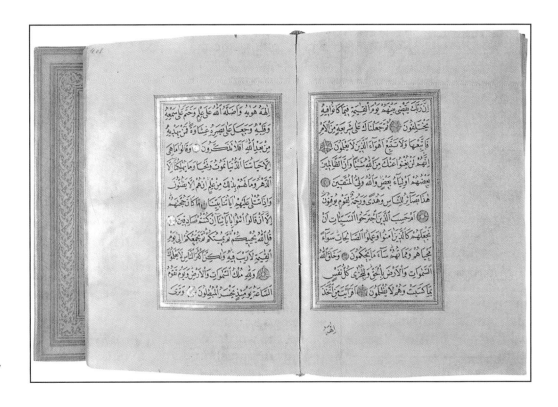

▶ *There are 2 original copies of the Qur'an in the world today. This copy is kept in Istanbul, Turkey*

Muslims treat the Qur'an with great respect. They wash themselves before reading it. They keep it wrapped up. They often put it on a high shelf to keep it safe.

Muslims should read the Qur'an every day. It is important to them because they believe it has the words of God. It teaches them about God and how he wants them to live. This is what one Muslim teenager said:

> It tells us what to do and what not to do. So that way we keep to the straight path. We've got the Qur'an to guide us and we've got the Prophet Muhammad's sayings.

This is what a young Muslim woman said was her favourite chapter of the Qur'an:

> I read Ya Sin every day. It helps make the day go by very easily. The Prophet encouraged Muslims to read this chapter regularly.

This is what an imam said (imams are the leaders at the mosques):

> We have a chapter called the Quraish. This is the name of the Prophet's own tribe. It mentions two main blessings – being free from hunger and free from fear. I find that these are the most important things in people's lives.

▲ *These copies of the Qur'an have been wrapped in cloth and placed on a shelf to protect them*

1 Copy and complete this paragraph:
The Muslim holy book is called the _____. Muslims believe it has the words of _____. It is written in the _____ language. Muhammad's own words are written in books called the _____.

2 Read again the quotations on this page. Explain in your own words why Muslims read the Qur'an.

3 The Qur'an gives people advice on how to live. They call it the Straight Path. In groups, talk about some good advice that you have been given.

4 Muslims take care of the Qur'an and read it regularly. Write down the best advice you have been given on a separate sheet of paper. Decorate it and put it on display in the classroom so that people can read it.

In this chapter we shall look at the things Muslims must believe. They should also act on these beliefs.

● One God (Allah)

Islam teaches that there is only one God. He has no partners or family. He is the only one people should worship. Every day, a Muslim says several times: 'There is no god but Allah and Muhammad is His Messenger.' It is also said when someone becomes a Muslim.

> O my dear son! Do not make any partner to Allah.
> Truly, making anyone partner to Allah is a big sin.
> *Qur'an 31 verse 13*

● His Angels

Muslims believe that angels are God's servants. They brought God's message to the prophets. They believe the angels keep a record of what we do. But we cannot see them.

● His Books

Islam teaches that God sent the prophets to guide us. They brought a number of holy books. For example, Moses brought the Law (the Torah) and Jesus the Gospels. But **they believe that only the Qur'an is God's full and correct message**. They believe it is for all people, for all time.

● His Prophets

The Qur'an names 25 prophets. The first was Adam; the last was Muhammad. **Muslims believe that the prophets were sent by God** to tell people how he wanted them to live.

● The Day of Judgment

Muslims believe that this is the day when God will judge people's lives. Those who have died will be brought back to life. Only God can judge, and only he can forgive.
Muhammad taught people that God would judge them on what they *intended* to happen:

> Actions shall be judged only by intention. A man shall get what he intends.
> *Hadith*

▲ *Muslims pray every day for forgiveness*

ISLAM

1 SHAHADAH — DECLARATION OF FAITH
2
3
4
5

لَا إِلَٰهَ إِلَّا اللَّهُ مُحَمَّدٌ رَسُولُ اللَّهِ

There is no god but Allah and Muhammad is His Messenger

▲ *Islam is like a house held up by 5 pillars. The first of these is that Muslims should declare their belief in God and Muhammad. This declaration of faith is called in Arabic, the 'Shahadah'.*

After the Day of Judgment, Islam teaches that some people will go to heaven and some to hell. Those who believe and obey God will go to heaven. They will be happy and at peace. Many who do not believe and do not obey God will go to hell. They will be miserable.

Islam teaches that only God can judge, because he is the only one who knows what is in people's hearts.

Muhammad teaches people to be humble if they want to go to heaven. (Paradise is another name for heaven.)

> If anyone has got an atom of pride in his heart, he will not enter Paradise.
>
> *Hadith*

1 Put the title 'The Five Pillars of Islam'. Draw the diagram above (without the Arabic!). Fill in the word BELIEF in the first pillar. Later in this chapter you will read about the other 4 pillars. You can fill these in when you come to them.

2 Muslims believe that the angels keep a record of what they do. Make your own record for the past week. Divide your page into 2 columns. In one, list all the good things you have done. In the other, list all the bad things.

3 Muhammad said that people will be judged on what they intended to happen
a) Are there any things in your list which you did not mean to do?
b) What do *you* think? Are intentions more important than what actually happens?

Key words

Shahadah
Arabic

● Beginning to Explore the Five Pillars

● 1 Belief

Letter	Arabic Pronunciation	Symbol
ا ب	alif	'
ت	ba'	b
	ta'	t
	tha'	s or t
	jīm	g or z
	Ha	H
	kha	kh
	dal	d
	thal	d or z
	ra	r
	za	z
	sīn	s
	shīn	sh
	sād	**s**
	dād	**d**
	tā	**t**
	thā	**z**
	ayn	"
	ghayn	gh
	fa'	f
	qāf	q or '
	kaf	k
	lam	l
	mīm	m
	nūn	n
	ha	h
	waw	w
	ya	yt

▲ Arabic letters are different from English letters

Do you remember the Muslim declaration of faith?

'There is no god but Allah, and Muhammad is His Messenger.'

See if your teacher can read it in Arabic:

'La illaha illal lahu. Muhammad rasulul la.'

This is what the first and last word looks like in Arabic writing:

"Lā"

▲ 'La' in Arabic

● 2 Prayer

SAUDI ARABIA

● Makkah

▲ Muslims pray towards Makkah

Do you remember that Muslims pray in the direction of the Ka'bah in Makkah? Many Muslims use a special compass so that they can know the direction of Makkah wherever they are.

3 Charity

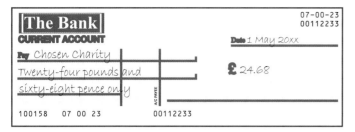

In pairs, add up how much money you get each week. Work out $\frac{1}{40}$ of the total (ie $2\frac{1}{2}$ pence for every pound). Draw a picture of a cheque. Write it out to the charity of your choice for that amount.

Muslims must donate at least $\frac{1}{40}$ th of their wealth to charity each year.

4 Fasting

▲ Fasting means to go without food. This café is closed!

Write a list of all the things you ate and drank today. Start from the morning until you went to sleep at night. Then cross out anything that you ate or drank while it was daylight.

Muslims must fast during the daylight hours of the month of Ramadan. So when do you think they eat and drink, to stay alive?

5 Pilgrimage

▲ A pop festival

Imagine you are going to a pop festival for the weekend. Make a list of all the things you would have to get ready beforehand (don't forget money to pay for it!). When something is important, we plan ahead and save up for it.

Going on pilgrimage is important to Muslims. A pilgrimage is a religious journey to a holy place. Muslims try to visit Makkah at least once in their life. This is so important to them that sometimes they save up for it all their life.

Prayer is very important for Muslims. It is a way to worship God who made them. It is a way to find God's guidance. It is a way to be washed clean of their sins.

Muslims must pray 5 times a day, 7 days a week. Their whole life is based on prayer. The call to prayer is the first thing a Muslim baby hears. It is the last thing spoken to a Muslim at death.

The 5 set daily prayers are called 'salah'. The diagram below shows when they come, and what they are called:

1 just after dawn
2 early afternoon
3 late afternoon
4 just after sunset
5 night time.

Muslims, of course, can say their own prayers at other times.

Prayers can be said in any space that is clean. They can be said at home, at work, at a station or airport. Men try to go to the mosque for prayers, if possible. This is very important for the early afternoon prayer on Fridays. Most prayers take about 10 minutes. But there is also a sermon at the Friday prayer.

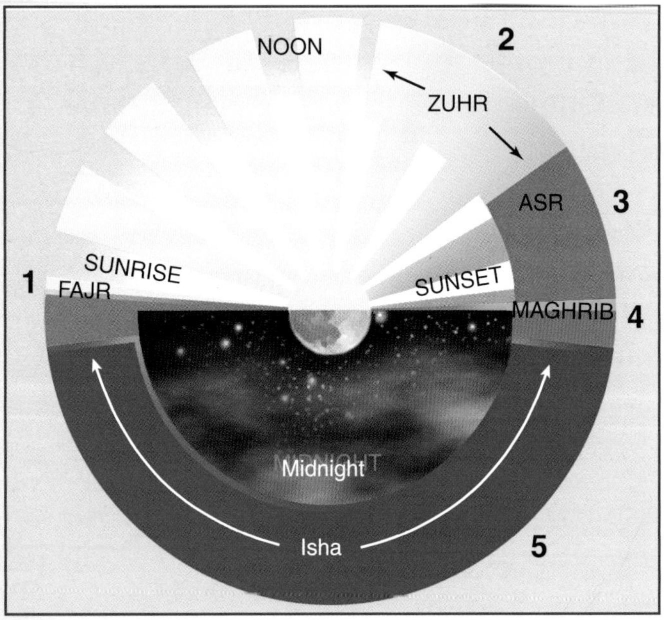

> There's quite a lot of Muslim boys in our school. We have a separate room to pray in. One of the mothers asked the headmaster for it. We only need to go there once a day for the afternoon prayer.
>
> *Darwa*

1 Draw a circle. Divide it in half, to show day and night, as on the diagram. Mark on it the 5 daily prayer times. (Use numbers rather than the Arabic names.)

2 Which prayer-time would you find most difficult? Explain why.

3 What can Muslims do if they cannot say their prayers at the correct time? Read what Ali does:

> There's nowhere in my school where I can go. So, at the end of the day, I just put my prayers together.

4 In class, read through the picture strips opposite. They show how Muslims prepare themselves for prayer. They also show what they do during prayer. Both women and men do this.

NOON **2**
ZUHR
ASR **3**
SUNRISE SUNSET
1 FAJR MAGHRIB **4**
Midnight
Isha **5**

◀ *The daily prayer times*

A Muslim must be clean. First, he washes

He says

In the name of Allah the most merciful, the most kind.

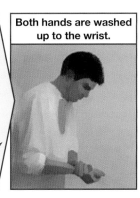

Both hands are washed up to the wrist.

The mouth is rinsed 3 times.

The nostrils and tip of the nose are washed 3 times.

The face is washed 3 times, from right to left and from forehead to throat.

Each arm is washed 3 times.

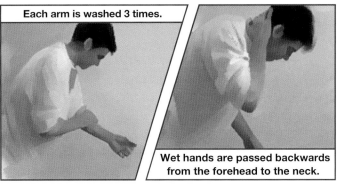

Wet hands are passed backwards from the forehead to the neck.

The ears and behind the ears are cleaned.

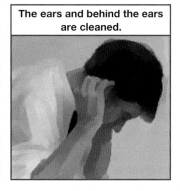

The neck is cleaned.

The feet are washed up to the ankles.

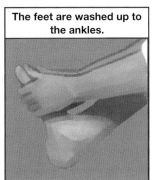

The Muslim says,

I bear witness that there is no God but Allah and I bear witness that Muhammad is his servant and messenger.

THE CALL TO PRAYER

After the call to prayer, everyone faces the Ka'bah in Makkah.

Each Muslim says how many prayers he intends to say.

Women's positions are slightly different.

Allahu Akbar.

(Allah is the greatest)

He recites the opening chapter of the Qur'an and any one other chapter.

O Allah, glory and praise are for you, and blessed is your name, and exalted is your majesty; there is no God but you. I seek shelter in Allah from the rejected Satan. In the name of Allah, the most merciful, the most kind.

Allahu Akbar. Glory to my Lord, the great.

(3 times)

Allah hears those who praise him. Our Lord praise be to you.

Allahu Akbar. Glory to my Lord, the highest.

(3 times)

Allahu Akbar.

He rests a moment, then prostrates himself on the floor again, repeating the words in the last picture.

Salah ends by repeating Allahu Akbar.

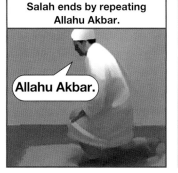

Allahu Akbar.

After Salah is complete, own prayers are said.

▼ *Muslims touch their heads to the ground when they pray.   This is called prostration*

Think of a peaceful place.   It might be somewhere you know, or somewhere in your imagination.   It is a place to be still, silent and alone.

Prayer for Muslims is partly about this feeling of peace.   A Muslim girl said:

> Saying my prayers and reading the Qur'an really makes me feel at peace.   It's good.

Another Muslim said that the 5 daily prayers were like tea breaks.   You looked forward to them during the day.   They were a break from work.   They made you feel refreshed.

Muslims express themselves in the prayer movements.   By touching their heads to the ground, they show complete obedience to God.   (Do you remember that 'Islam' can mean 'obey'?)

1 What does it mean to bow to someone? (This is one of the prayer positions.)

2 What does it mean when a Muslim kneels and puts his or her head on the ground?

3 What do you think it means when someone prays with cupped hands?

◄ *What would aliens make of our places of worship?*

Imagine that aliens landed on Earth and saw the different religions at worship. They returned to their planet with descriptions of the buildings that were used. These are 2 of them. Can you tell which is the mosque?

1 A building with a tall pointed tower with a cross on the top, coloured glass in the windows, fixed rows of wooden seats and a special area at one end around a table.

2 A building with a dome and a tall tower, a moon on top of the dome, an area for washing, no seats and a decorated alcove on one wall.

The Muslim place of worship is called a mosque. This means 'place of prostration'. So, it is a clean place where Muslims can bend low before God. You remember that prostration is when a person kneels forward and touches the ground with their forehead.

The photo below shows a large mosque in Regent's Park in London. Not all mosques are as big as this. Some are in ordinary houses.

1 Draw an outline of a mosque with a dome and tall tower.

▲ *Can you see: 1 The mihrab – the alcove which points the way to Makkah; 2 The minbar – the stand for the sermon to be preached from; 3 The space for prayer movements; 4 The beautiful decorations – especially the patterns*

The tall tower is called a minaret. This is used to call people to prayer. The Arabic words carry across the rooftops. This is what it means in English:

Allah is the greatest, Allah is the greatest
Allah is the greatest, Allah is the greatest
I bear witness that there is no God but Allah
I bear witness that there is no God but Allah
I bear witness that Muhammad is Allah's messenger
I bear witness that Muhammad is Allah's messenger
Rush to prayer, rush to prayer,
Rush to success, rush to success,
Allah is the greatest, Allah is the greatest
There is no God but Allah

If you ever visit a Muslim country, you will probably hear the call to prayer. It might wake you up in the morning!

As well as the alcove and raised platform, mosques must have the following:
● somewhere for men and women to wash
● somewhere for people to leave their shoes. Muslims always take off their shoes before going into the prayer hall. It is important to keep the floor clean because they put their foreheads on the ground.

There is very little furniture. Muslims need space for the prayer movements. The floor is usually carpeted for them to kneel and sit down.

Key words

minaret	mihrab
calligraphy	minbar
prostration	

◀ *This is over the door to a mosque. It is beautifully decorated with words from the Qur'an and patterns*

Muhammad stopped people praying to idols. He was afraid they might go back to worshipping them. So no statues or paintings of humans or animals are allowed in mosques. Instead, Muslims decorate their mosques with words from the Qur'an. These are written in beautiful writing, called calligraphy. Mosques are also decorated with patterns.

Muslims go to mosques to pray to God. Nothing should take their mind off him. Therefore men and women worship separately, so that they can think only of God.

This man came across some Muslims getting ready for prayer:

> As we walked along the hot dusty road, we heard a voice fill the air. The words fell upon our ears, 'Allahu Akbar' (Allah is the greatest).
>
> Now we saw many people coming together. They spread long mats on the ground. The people took off their shoes and sandals. They formed long lines, one line behind the other.
>
> We were amazed that there were white men, yellow men and black men. There were poor men and rich men, beggars and merchants. They were all standing side by side. Not one single person looked away from the mat in front of him.

33

1 Draw the inside of a mosque. Label the minbar and mihrab.

2 Imagine that some Muslims are coming to talk to your class about prayer. Make a list of SEVEN questions you might ask them. Then ask your teacher to tell you what answers they would give.

3 This chapter started with an alien's description of a mosque (see page 31). From what you know about a mosque, do you think this is a good enough report to send back to an alien leader? Write your own, better, report about what a mosque is.

There are no priests in Islam. There are religious leaders called imams. This word means 'at the front'. An imam is the prayer leader who stands at the front of the others. They are chosen because they are good Muslims who know their religion well.

▲ *An imam at a mosque in Manchester*

This is how one imam describes his work:

> An imam does a lot of things. As well as sermons, I lead the prayers and advise people. I visit bereaved people, sick people and sometimes people in prison. I start very early and end very late.

The imam's day starts with morning prayer. This can be as early as 3 am. Then he will read the Qur'an before breakfast. He may then rest before his day's work.

Many imams do this in their spare time. They earn their money in another full-time job. Only the big mosques can afford to pay imams.

This is how another full-time imam describes his work:

> I am in charge of religion at the mosque, education, money and the building. I run the Islamic school for children every evening and mid-week classes for other groups. I visit many schools and speak about Islam to many non-Muslim groups. I am also the Muslim chaplain at the local prison and hospitals.

Many mosques run Islamic schools. Muslim children go there to learn about their religion. They learn to read the Qur'an in Arabic. Some mosques run them every evening – but not this one:

> They come only one day a week, at weekends. I don't think 3 to 4 hours a week is enough. But it would be a bit much to come to the mosque at the end of a long day at school.
>
> *Imam at the London Central Mosque*

Friday is a special day at the mosque. The Arabic word for Friday means 'Day of Assembly'. It is the day when Muslim men, at least, should go to the mosque for their early afternoon prayers. (Women may stay at home if they have young children to care for.)

The imam preaches a sermon at this time. It has 2 parts. First, he recites from the Qur'an. Then he explains what it means. It is also a chance to talk about Islam and things that are happening in the world.

Afterwards, Muslims go back to work. It is not a day of rest.

◀ *Children learning about Islam in a religious school at a mosque*

In pairs:

1 a) Look at the quotation boxes and list TWELVE things imams do.
b) Which of the jobs do you think is most important for an imam? Explain why.

2 Write an advert for an imam. You will need to think about:
- Will it be a full-time job or not?
- What sort of person do you want?
- What will he have to do?

3 a) Why do mosques run Islamic schools for their children?
b) What difficulties might there be for Muslim children in this country who go to Islamic school every evening after normal school?

> He is not a believer who eats his fill while his neighbour remains hungry by his side.
>
> *Muhammad in the Hadith*

Islam has clear teaching about wealth:

- Everything belongs to God.
- Everything people have comes from God.
- People should make money honestly.
- People should use their money as God would wish.

This means that they should not waste their money. Nor should they be greedy and hold onto their money. They should share what they have with those in need.

If they do this, it is a way of thanking God for what they have.

Zakah (charity) helps Muslims to do this. **Zakah is the third pillar of Islam. It is a $\frac{1}{40}$ th tax on wealth. It helps spread the wealth from the rich to the poor.** Look at the pictures below to see how the money may be spent.

Zakah is usually paid once a year. In Islamic countries, it is collected by the government. Elsewhere, it is usually collected at the mosques.

A Muslim can give zakah direct to another person. But most prefer to give it secretly. Then the giver will not feel proud, and the poorer person will not be embarrassed. Muhammad said:

> The best charity is that which the right hand gives and the left hand does not know about.

 **1** The poor and needy	 **2** People who have recently become Muslims	 **3** Prisoners-of-war	 **4** People in debt
 **5** Muslim tax collectors (for wages)	 **6** Muslims studying Islam	 **7** Travellers who need help	 **8** Hospitals, schools, libraries and mosques

▲ *The Qur'an sets out who may receive zakah*

Zakah is a duty for Muslims. They expect to give it. They believe that poor people have a right to this money.

So it is not like normal charity. It is not like putting a coin in a tin on a flag day. Muslims can give to these charities as well as zakah, if they wish.

A British Muslim explains how it works:

We collect our zakah among ourselves. Then we seek out any Muslim who needs help. For instance, a mother whose husband has died, and she has many children. She may not have enough money to buy clothes for her children. But it is left to a Muslim's conscience. Nobody comes round asking, 'How much do you earn? How much have you got in the bank?' If you cheat, you're cheating yourself. You will have to answer to God on the Day of Judgment. You will have to explain why you were so mean, why you didn't pay your charity out of the money that God gave you.

▲ *A Muslim mother teaches her children to give zakah*

Key word

zakah

1 Read Chapter 12 and answer these questions:
  a) What is zakah?
  b) Why do Muslims pay zakah?
  c) How is it given in Britain?

2 Look at the pictures on page 36. Talk about why each of these people need help:
  a) a traveller abroad
  b) people in debt
  c) students of Islam.

3 a) Do you think we should give to charity? Explain your answer.
  b) Do you think it is helpful to be told how much to give?
  c) Do you have a favourite charity? If so, what is it, and why do you think it should be supported?

To fast means to go without food. **Once a year, during the month of Ramadan, Muslims must fast.** They go without food and drink during daylight hours. This is the fourth pillar of Islam.

Why do Muslims fast in Ramadan?
- The Qur'an tells them to.
- Ramadan is a special month. Muslims believe that it was in this month that Muhammad was first given verses of the Qur'an.
- Muhammad himself kept the fast.

How does fasting help Muslims?
- It makes them thankful for their food and drink.
- They understand the poor better.
- They learn self-control.
- They think more about God.

If you look at the pictures on this page, you will see that fasting is only for those who are fit and strong. Most children want to fast because everyone else is doing it. Parents will help them to fast a little at a time. They do not have to do the full fast until they are adults.

Two Muslim boys talk about fasting:

- You feel for the poor and hungry. You're only fasting for a day. You're going to eat food at sunset. But they feel hungry all the time.

  In the beginning you feel hungry, but then you get used to it. I went to school and I did athletics. I didn't feel anything because I got used to it.

- You start feeling a bit hungry about 4 o'clock. But if you start feeling hungry, you read the Qur'an.

▼ *Not everyone has to fast*

You do not have to fast if…

You are a child

You are too old

You are pregnant or feeding a baby

You are travelling more than 50 miles

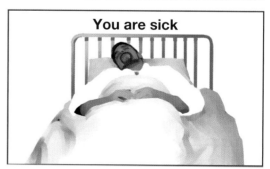

You are sick

38

◀ *This Muslim family shares a good breakfast before the daily fast begins*

Muslims usually have a meal before dawn during the month of Ramadan. Even so, it is not easy to go all day without food and drink. It might be tempting to hide somewhere and have a quick snack! But Muslims believe that God sees everything they do.

At the end of the day, they break their fast with a light snack. Later they have a big meal. They share their food with the poor.

Ramadan is not just about giving things up. Muslims spend more time on their religion at this time. They read the Qur'an and pray. They try to live as God wants them to.

One night in Ramadan is specially important. It is called the 'Night of Power'. Muslims believe that the Qur'an was first given to Muhammad on this night. Many Muslims try to stay awake on this night. They read the Qur'an and say extra prayers.

> Better is the Night of Power than 1000 months . . . That night is peace, till the break of day.
>
> *Qur'an 79 verses 3–5*

1 Match up the words with their correct meanings:

Ramadan	Muslim holy book
sawm	special month
Qur'an	fasting

2 Talk about why the people in the pictures on page 38 do not have to fast.

3 Think about these questions:
a) Do you think you appreciate the food and drink you have every mealtime?
b) Have you ever gone without food? Has this made you appreciate it more?

4 Write a short article for a mosque newsletter for the month of Ramadan. Explain in your article why Muslims should fast.

Five times a day Muslims turn towards the Ka'bah in Makkah when they pray. This is the centre of Islam. They believe it was the first place of worship of the 'one God'. It was also where Muhammad lived much of his life. So it is a very important place for Muslims.

The fifth pillar of Islam is pilgrimage to Makkah. It is called the hajj. All Muslims should try to do this pilgrimage at least once in their lifetime. In practice, about one in 10 manage it. Some Muslims save up all their lives to do it.

The hajj takes place at a particular time each year. At this time, about 2 million pilgrims arrive in Makkah in Saudi Arabia. They come from all over the world.

Before they reach Makkah, they change into their pilgrim clothes. These are 2 simple white sheets for the men. One is tied round the waist. The other is thrown over the shoulder. Women can wear any clothes, but must cover everything except their hands and faces.

This dress is important. It makes all the pilgrims equal. There is no difference between rich and poor. It shows that they are all equal in the eyes of God. It also reminds the pilgrims that they have left behind their ordinary lives. They are here to think only about God.

40

Key words

hajj
hajji
hajja

▲ Muslims on hajj, wearing white sheets

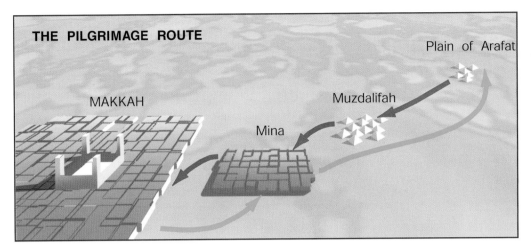

THE PILGRIMAGE ROUTE

Plain of Arafat

MAKKAH

Muzdalifah

Mina

◀ Use this diagram to find each place as it is mentioned on this page

● Makkah

- Here pilgrims walk 7 times around the Ka'bah. This is the building in the centre of the Great Mosque in Makkah. It is covered in a black cloth.
- Then they jog between 2 small hills. They do this in memory of a story about Hagar, the mother of Ishmael. She ran between the hills, searching for water. Meanwhile the baby dug his heels into the sands and found a spring of water.

● Arafat

- The most important day of the hajj is spent here. It is some way out from Makkah, in the desert. Thousands of tents are put up to protect the pilgrims from the heat. They spend part of the time on a small hill called the Mount of Mercy. Here they ask God to forgive their sins. They spend the night at Muzdalifah.

● Mina

- There are 3 stone pillars here. Pilgrims throw stones at them. It is called stoning the devil. It shows they want to drive away evil.
- They celebrate a festival here called Id-ul-Adha. Animals are killed as an offering to God. Some of the meat is eaten, and the rest is given for the poor.

Back in Makkah, pilgrims visit the Ka'bah once more. Some go on from here to Madinah, the town of Prophet Muhammad.

▲ The decorations on this house in Egypt show that the owner has been on the hajj. Such a man is called a hajji; a woman is called a hajja

One hajji says what it felt like to go on hajj. He said that the pilgrims often worry about doing everything correctly. They study it all beforehand.

You find yourself moved and touched. You have become a very small part of a great assembly. Sometimes you don't worry about the details of the order of events. . . it is good to know what steps to do but, as far as feeling them, that can only be got by going there. It is an amazing experience.

41

▲ *Malcolm X*

All the things that the pilgrims have to do on hajj are done for these reasons:

- to show respect (circling the Ka'bah)
- to remember God's care (jogging between the hills)
- to turn away from evil (stoning the pillars)
- to offer something to God (killing an animal).

Muslims on hajj are reminded that they are all equal in the eyes of God. This became clear to one black Muslim leader from the USA. His name was Malcolm X.

It was in the 1960s. He had joined a black Muslim movement to protest against the poor conditions of black Americans. He saw the white man as the enemy, the very devil.

But when he made his first hajj, he was changed. Here were Muslims of all races, side by side, helping each other and praying together. Once he sat between 2 white men. He had to accept a sip of water from one and share the cup with the other. This changed Malcolm X's views. He made up his mind that, when he returned to America, he would work with anyone who would help – white or black.

1 Put these events from the hajj in their correct order:

- stoning the pillars at Mina
- putting on pilgrim dress
- celebrating Id-ul-Adha
- praying at Arafat
- jogging between the 2 hills
- walking 7 times round the Ka'bah
- spending the night at Muzdalifah.

2 Your teacher will divide the class into 4 groups, and give each group ONE of these tasks. Think about times when:

a) you felt respect for someone

b) you needed help, and someone cared for you

c) you turned away from something you knew was wrong

d) you gave something valuable to another person.

Each group should make a display on their task, on a large sheet of paper. They should use this to talk to the rest of the class about their ideas.

● Birth

Muslims have 6 things that they do when a baby is born.

1 The first words spoken to a new-born baby are the call to prayer (on page 32). This shows that its parents want the child to grow up as a Muslim. They want the child to put God first in his or her life.

2 A small piece of softened date or honey is rubbed around the baby's gums. This shows that they wish the child a sweet and happy life.

3 At 7 days old, the baby's hair is shaved off. The parents pay an equal weight in silver or gold to the poor. Sometimes much more is given. This is a way of thanking God for the gift of the child. It is also a way of sharing their happiness with others.

4 The child is then given a Muslim name.

5 Muslim boys are usually circumcised soon after birth. This often takes place at 7 days.

6 A meal is served to friends and neighbours. Usually a lamb or goat is killed for this. Some of the meat is given to the poor.

This is what happens at one British mosque:

> The father will bring the food and will invite everybody in the mosque to join in. Naturally, there will be many people. Some will be poor people, although they may not be as poor as in some countries.

43

Key word
circumcised

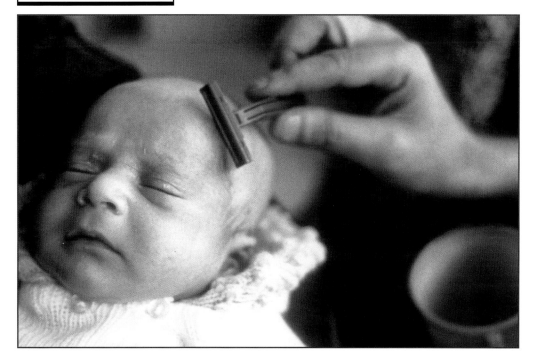

◀ *The baby's head is shaved*

● Death

▶ *A Muslim funeral*

Death is always sad. Parting from loved ones is never easy. But Muslims believe in life after death. They believe that they will meet their loved ones again one day.

When a Muslim is close to death, he or she will repeat: 'There is no god but Allah, and Muhammad is his prophet.' After death, the body is washed and wrapped in white cloths. If the dead person had made the hajj, then his white pilgrim clothes are used.

> If the law of the country says that people must be buried in a coffin, then we obey that law. It is a matter of custom rather than religion. What is important is to show respect for the dead.

Burial takes place as soon as possible. Cremation is not allowed. Muslims try to bury the body so that the face points towards the Ka'bah. As the earth is put over the body, people say these words from the Qur'an: 'We created you from it and put you into it and from it We will take you out once more.'

Muhammad taught that a good Muslim will leave behind 3 gifts for others:
1 possessions
2 knowledge
3 an example of how to live.

1 Which TWO birth ceremonies show that Muslims care for the poor?

2 a) List THREE gifts a good Muslim should leave behind after death.

b) Talk in class about who could benefit from each of these gifts.

c) What do you think is the most important of the 3 gifts? Explain why.

d) What would you like people to remember about you?

44

> O mankind, be mindful of your duty to your Lord who created you from a single soul and from it created its mate and from the two created many men and women.
>
> *Qur'an 4 verse 1*

Marriage is very important in Islam. Most of the prophets, including Muhammad, were married. The Qur'an says that Muslims ought to marry.

Islam gives rights to both men and women in marriage. A Muslim wife keeps her own name after marriage. Any property she owned before marriage remains hers. Muhammad, in the Hadith, said:

> 'How can you beat your wife like a camel, when a moment later you will make love to her?'

Muslim marriages are different from most Western marriages because usually the parents try to find a suitable bride and groom.

> **MW916**: 19-year-old Moroccan computer student, kind-natured, seeks religious Muslim wife.
>
> **MW911**: Scottish Muslim, 18 years old, training as nurse, 5ft 7in, likes writing, seeks lifelong partner.

▲ *Adverts like these are placed in newspapers and magazines by Muslim parents*

This is known as arranged marriage. Love comes after the couple get married, not before. The couple do have some say in it. They must agree before the marriage goes ahead. But most youngsters trust their parents to choose for them. After all, their parents know about marriage.

45

◄ *A muslim wedding – the bride and groom*

▶ *A Muslim bride signs her marriage contract*

This Muslim woman describes how her marriage was arranged:

> I was about to go to university to start my law degree. My mother felt that it was not acceptable for a young single woman to go away from home. She felt that marriage would provide a kind of wall round me, saying, 'Keep off. Married.' So I was married. It was an arranged marriage. I knew my husband already and we got on pretty well.

When the marriage is decided the 2 sets of parents will fix the marriage contract. This includes a dowry. This is money or jewellery given by the man to his future wife. She owns this and can do with it what she pleases.

Muslim weddings are simple, although everyone wears their best clothes. The marriage can take place at a mosque or at the bride's house. Two witnesses must be present. There may be a reading from the Qur'an. The next day, the bridegroom gives a feast for their relatives and friends.

Islam allows men to marry up to 4 wives. But this is rare. Muhammad said that a man must treat each wife equally and very few Muslims can afford to do this.

Muslims are allowed to divorce, but it is not liked. The couple are helped to sort out their problems first. The Hadith says: 'Of all the lawful things, the one which God dislikes most is divorce.'

1 Answer these questions in sentences:
   a) What is an arranged marriage?
   b) What is a dowry and who pays it?
   c) Where do Muslim marriages take place?
   d) What does Islam teach about divorce?

2 Your teacher will divide the class in half. One half will think about the advantages of arranged marriage. The other will think of the disadvantages. (It will be easier if you work in smaller groups, and jot down your ideas.) After discussing your ideas in class, draw 2 columns in your work-book and make your own list of advantages and disadvantages.

3 If you could choose your marriage partner, what sort of person would you choose?

Family life is important in Islam. The Qur'an lays down clear guidelines. It says that parents must be kind to their children, and children must be kind to their parents. Read what Muhammad said:

> Man: Who deserves the best care from me?
> Muhammad: Your mother.
> Man: Who else after that?
> Muhammad: Your mother.
> Man: Who else?
> Muhammad: Your mother.
> Man: Then who else?
> Muhammad: Your father.

As they grow older, parents may need to be looked after by their children. This may mean having the parents to live with them, or helping them out with money. This duty continues until the parents die.

Above all, parents expect their children to obey them. This is a duty, partly in return for all that the parents do for their children.

> Your Lord has ordered that you worship none but Him and show kindness to your parents . . . Never be harsh with them, but speak to them kindly. And serve them with tenderness and humility and say, 'My Lord, have mercy on them, just as they cared for me as a little child.'
>
> *Qur'an 17 verses 23–24*

However, parents are not always right. Children should also be aware of what God wishes. If they have to choose between their parents or God, they should obey God.

Muslim boys and girls are expected to work hard at school and do well. Muslims believe that education makes good people. As a result, Muslims tend to obey the law. An imam said this:

> The Qur'an says that children must respect their parents and be kind to them. This is always hammered home, especially in Western countries, with the sense of freedom here.

▲ *This Muslim family worships together in their home*

47

◄ *A Muslim woman
with her grandchild*

Parents have to set an example. Where three generations live together, the grandchild will see how his father is treating *his* father. Of course, I can't say all children are obedient to their parents, but I think that Muslims are more fortunate than others.

Shaikh Gamal Solaiman

Parents too have duties to their children. Muhammad liked children and wanted Muslims to be kind to children. The Qur'an makes it clear that every child has a right to be treated equally.

Orphans are cared for within Muslim families. If there are no relatives, then other Muslims should take on this task.

Muslims often live in extended families. This means that grandparents, parents and children live together in the same house. Sometimes there are other relatives too. Or sometimes they live in the same street.

People used to live in extended families in the West. They used to get married and live in the area where they grew up. But people now often move away for work.

There are pros and cons in living in an extended family. Can you think of any?

1 a) How do you treat your parents?
b) How would they like to be treated?
c) If you had children, how would you like them to treat you?

2 In pairs talk about these statements:
Muslim children should:
● obey their parents
● be kind to them, and
● look after them in their old age.
Do you agree with each of these?

3 If your grandparents came to live with you, how would your life be better, and how would it be worse?

▲ *Muslim teenage girls in modest clothes*

Muslim parents tend to be strict with their children. They often do not like them going to parties and clubs. This is because they do not want boys and girls to mix freely, and Muslims are not allowed to drink alcohol. They do not approve of boyfriends and girlfriends. Sex outside marriage is forbidden.

These rules can be a problem for Muslims living in non-Muslim countries like Britain. Many Muslim teenagers want the same freedoms as their non-Muslim friends. This can start arguments at home. But some Muslim parents have become more Westernised, and accept current fashions.

1 Work out ONE of these role-plays:
  a) A Muslim girl tries to persuade her mother to let her wear Western clothes.
  b) A Muslim boy is out with some non-Muslim friends and they start drinking.

▲ *Many Muslim teenagers would not be allowed to do these things. Can you say why?*

Westerners often think that Muslim women are not treated equally to men. In fact, Islam teaches the opposite. At the time of Muhammad, women were bought and sold like possessions. But Muhammad gave them an important place. He said, 'Paradise lies at the feet of your mothers.'

Islam teaches that men and women are equal, but they have different duties. The man's duty is to go out to work and take part in public affairs. The woman's duty is to look after the home and care for her family. This does not mean that a Muslim woman may not work outside her home. Many Muslim women are teachers and doctors. In farming villages, both men and women share the work.

▲ *A Muslim woman with her face covered in public*

> During the time of the Prophet, women worked. I can see no problem, according to the Qur'an. They have equal legal rights. This is what Islam gives the woman in theory. But in practice you find it is quite different.
>
> *Egyptian woman*

This Egyptian woman points out that what Islam teaches is not always what happens. It depends to a large extent on the customs and laws of the countries where they live. In Saudi Arabia, for example, women are not allowed to go out alone. They are not allowed to drive cars. Most live their lives in their close family circle. Yet some go to university and have important jobs. There is even a women's bank, run by women for women customers only.

The Qur'an gives advice about clothing. It teaches Muslims to dress decently in public. Men should not be too dressy. They should dress modestly, covering themselves from the waist to the knees. Women should also dress modestly. They should cover themselves up and not show off their figures. This will stop women tempting men and from being gossiped about.

Muslim dress often causes difficulties in non-Muslim countries. An imam explains the difficulties of mixed swimming:

> A Muslim girl can go swimming with other girls. She can go in a swimming costume with girls and a lady instructor. But swimming with men would be a problem.

There are different styles of Muslim dress in different countries. Asian Muslim women often wear suits of baggy trousers and long tunics. In Iran, women wear long black gowns in public. Some Muslim women believe they have to cover their faces too.

However, inside her own home, a Muslim woman can dress as she likes. Islam does not stop her from dressing up and making herself attractive to her husband. It only tries to protect her from strangers.

- The Muslim girl has to come to terms with the fact that she's different. My parents encouraged me to wear trousers. Although I looked very odd in the beginning, I told the other girls at school why I had to wear them and that they should respect me as I respected what they were wearing as well.

- I'm not an object that needs to be admired or looked at. Muslim women don't want to have to sell their looks to be heard. We want to be listened to for what we have to say.

- When I was 9, my parents wanted me to wear this scarf. I used to go to school with it, and I hated it. When I was 12, I used to feel deeply ashamed. But when I was 18, I started to like wearing it. I felt proud of it.

▲ *These Muslim women are wearing the national dress of Pakistan*

1 In groups:

Cut out pictures and articles from newspapers and magazines about *either* men *or* women. Make a poster showing our society's view of men or women. Put them up on display.

2 In pairs:

a) In what ways are men and women equal in our society?

b) In what ways are they different?

c) Do you think they should be equal?

3 Make a list of the difficulties for Muslim girls growing up in non-Muslim countries?

Human beings need to celebrate special events. They throw parties and share food and drink. They visit their families and give gifts. We need some fun in life. We need things to look forward to. When we remember birthdays and other special events, it helps us to value them.

Religions have festivals too. **Islam has 2 main festivals. They are called Id-ul-Fitr and Id-ul-Adha.** (The Muslim word for 'festival' is 'id'.)

▲ *We need some fun in life*

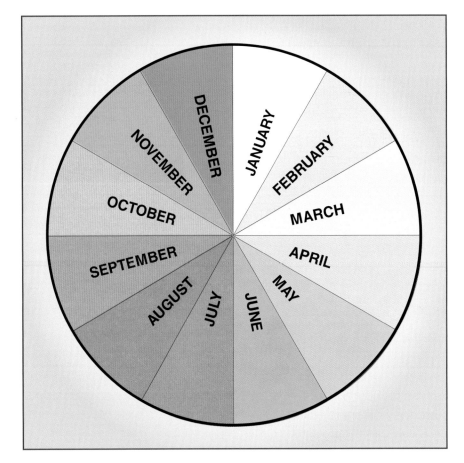

▲ *A year's calendar*

1 Copy this chart on a page of your book. Write in any special events that your family celebrates. Holidays could be included if you go at the same time each year.

◀ *These goats have been specially fattened and decorated to be sacrificed*

The two main Muslim festivals are national holidays in Muslim countries. They are times of great joy for Muslims all over the world. They dress up in their best clothes. They get together with friends and relatives. They share food and give cards and presents. But they are not just for fun. They are times to remember God and give him thanks. They begin with prayers at the mosque.

● Id-ul-Fitr

This festival comes at the end of Ramadan. Muslims thank God for helping them to fast during Ramadan. They enjoy the festival food. They give to the poor to make sure that they too can share in the feast. They also thank God for giving them the Qur'an.

> Ramadan – we take it as it comes, as part of life. At Id, everybody gives each other presents. That's probably the favourite festival.

● Id-ul-Adha

This festival comes at the end of the time of the hajj (the pilgrimage to Makkah). It is the festival of sacrifice. It recalls a famous story about Abraham. Abraham was ready to kill his son Ishmael because he believed God wanted this sacrifice. But God did not let Abraham kill his son. He gave him a sheep to sacrifice instead.

When Muslims kill animals at this festival, they are showing that they too are ready to give their lives to God. The meat is shared with friends and relatives and, of course, the poor.

Key words

id
Id-ul-Fitr
Id-ul-Adha
sacrifice

▲ These boys from Kenya are dancing to celebrate Muhammad's birthday

▲ An id card. Notice the Arabic writing and the beautiful decorations

A British Muslim describes Id-ul-Adha:

> My feelings were of joy. It was a day to celebrate what Abraham did many years ago. It was a day when I could join with thousands of other people in worshipping God. It was a day to ask for forgiveness, and to know that my prayers were answered.

Apart from these 2 main festivals, Muslims also celebrate these events in Muhammad's life:

● his birthday
● the Night of Power – during the month of Ramadan, when the Qur'an was first given to Muhammad.

1 Match up these festivals and events:

Id-ul-Fitr   sacrifice of animals
Night of Power   the end of fasting
Id-ul-Adha   the giving of the Qur'an

2 Unless you are vegetarian, feasts involve the killing of animals for meat. Is this any different from the sacrifice of animals at Id-ul-Adha? Talk about this.

3 Make an id card. Use the one in the picture for ideas. Think about:
● Which way will it open?
● Why won't it have pictures of people or animals on it?
● What greeting might a Muslim put in it? (Think about what the festival is celebrating.)

Say Allah's name (Bismillah) and eat with your right hand and eat from near you.

A vital part of everyday life is food. We have seen that Muslims fast during Ramadan. **They also have rules about what they can eat at other times.** After all, food affects our health; and Islam wants a healthy society. So Muslims can eat and drink anything that is pure and good – but not too much of it.

Halal is the food they can eat.

Haram is the food they cannot eat.

▲ *Muslims try to buy their food from halal shops*

55

> **Key words**
>
> halal   haram

Halal meat is killed in the name of God. Also, Muslims believe that the animal is killed more kindly than by other methods. The animal is separated from the others, so as not to cause distress to the others. It is approached from behind, so as not to frighten it. The knife is so sharp that the cut is swift and not felt. This is very different from Western abattoirs, where animals are herded together and pushed around.

There are some other rules:

- Muslims can eat fish and vegetables
- they must not eat anything from pigs, even lard
- they must not eat anything that is already dead
- they must not eat animals which eat meat themselves.

They're considered to be bad for the body. Anything that is bad for the body is also bad for the spirit as well.

Muslims should not drink alcohol or take drugs. Muslims want a healthy society. Alcohol can lead to drunkenness and trouble. Muslim countries like Saudi Arabia ban the sale of alcohol.

> O you who believe, wine and gambling . . . are filthy tricks of Satan; avoid them so that you may prosper. Satan wants to make . . . hatred among you by means of wine and gambling and prevent you from remembering Allah and from Salah. So will you not give them up?
>
> *Qur'an 5 verses 90–91*

Muslims thank God, and wash, before and after meals. The eldest member of the family eats first, unless there is a guest. No one leaves the table until everyone has finished.

It can be difficult to get halal food in a non-Muslim country. Some British schools with Muslim children now provide halal food for them. But if a Muslim cannot get halal food, then they can eat other food. Islam is a very practical religion. It does not insist on things that can't be done. Personal survival must come first.

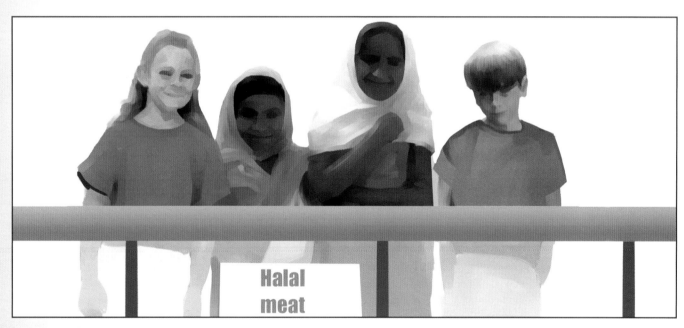

Halal meat

▲ *Some schools have halal food for Muslim children to eat*

1 a) In a class discussion, collect ideas on the dangers of drinking alcohol.

b) Working in groups, take ONE idea in each group and design a TV ad to put it across.

2 a) Are there any foods which you will not eat? Make a list, and put the reason beside each.

b) What do you think a vegetarian should do if they went to a barbecue where there was only meat to eat?

There are many Muslim countries in the world today. They all follow Islam. If they acted together, they would be a powerful force. Yet on some matters they disagree. **One disagreement within Islam goes back to its very early days. It has led to the 2 main branches of Islam:**

1 The Sunnis

Most Muslims in the world are Sunnis. Their name means 'path'. They believe they are following the right path. Major Arab nations like Saudi Arabia are Sunni.

2 The Shi'ites

Their name means 'group'. They broke away from the Sunnis soon after Muhammad's death. They claim that Muhammad appointed his son-in-law, Ali, to succeed him, not Abu Bakr. Their leaders are the descendants of Ali.

▼ *A Shi'ite shrine in Syria*

There are far fewer Shi'ites than Sunnis. So they have never had as much power as the Sunnis. But this changed towards the end of the 20th century. Iran is the main home of the Shi'ite Muslims. In 1979 there was a revolution in Iran. It was led by a religious leader called Ayatollah Khomeini. He brought back many Islamic laws and customs. For example, alcohol was banned, and women had to cover themselves up in public.

▲ *The festival of Ashura marks the death of Ali's son, Husayn, in battle. Some men injure themselves at this festival. Shi'ite Muslims have special respect for those who are prepared to suffer and die for their religion*

▲ *Ayatollah Khomeini. 'Ayatollah' means 'Sign of God'. It is the title given to religious leaders in Iran*

1 Answer these questions in sentences:
   a) What are the TWO main Muslim groups?
   b) Which group is the larger?
   c) What did the Shi'ite and Sunni disagree about?
   d) Name ONE Sunni country and ONE Shi'ite country.

2 a) Read the caption about the festival of Ashura. Why do you think Shi'ite Muslims want to suffer at this festival?
   b) Are there any special dates when *you* remember something sad that has happened? Share them with a partner if you want to.

● The growth of Islam

No one knows exactly how many Muslims there are in the world today. We do know that Islam is the second largest religion after Christianity. Many Western people have become Muslims in recent years.

Islam began to grow in the second half of the 20th century. For 200 years before that, most Muslim countries were under Western control. After the Second World War, they gained their independence. Many became rich from selling their oil.

In 1973, Arab countries got together and used their oil as a weapon. It happened when Israel was at war with Egypt and Syria. Israel is a Jewish country, and was supported by the USA. Egypt and Syria are Arab countries. They were supported by most other Muslim countries. The Arab countries stopped selling oil to the USA. The result was a world oil shortage. Almost overnight, prices trebled! The Arabs had a powerful weapon, and the West was forced to take them seriously.

● The Iran/Iraq War

Islam would be a more powerful force in the world, if all Muslim countries worked together. But there are divisions. The war between Iran and Iraq from 1980 to 1988 is an example of this. These two Muslim countries are neighbours, but also enemies.

Iran is a Shi'ite country. Iraq is Sunni, even though more than half the Iraqi people are Shi'ite. After the revolution of 1979 (see page 58), Iran wanted Shi'ites in other countries to fight for power, too. Iraq did not want this to happen, and went to war with Iran. The war finally ended, but not until hundreds of thousands of soldiers had been killed. Some of these were just boys.

▲ *Iranian soldiers at prayer during the war with Iraq*

After the 1979 revolution in Iran, a lot of people voted to set up an Islamic state there. This means that it is ruled by the religious leaders, and the laws are based on the Qur'an. This is like the Islamic state that Muhammad himself ruled from Madinah.

In an Islamic state, there is no difference between religion and politics. Religion governs the whole way of life. It means that women must dress modestly, following Islamic rules. It means that no alcohol is sold there. It means that physical punishments are given, such as flogging, and cutting off the hand of a person who will not stop stealing. The death penalty is also used for certain crimes. These punishments hit our headlines when Westerners are involved. But Muslims claim that they have far less crime than Western countries.

Iran would like to see all Muslim countries run like this. Countries such as Saudi Arabia and Pakistan have Islamic laws. Other Muslim countries, like Turkey, are less strict.

1 List THREE ways in which religion affects life in Iran.

2 Think about how religion influences our society. Think about:
- RE and worship in schools
- important times in people's lives
- the main festivals each year
- how religion comes into TV programmes
- examples of religion in the news

Write a paragraph (like the one above on Iran) on how religion affects the way of life in our society.

◀ *Women in Iran cover their faces in public*

◀ *Some Muslim instruments for maths and science*

The Qur'an encourages Muslims to seek knowledge. Their religion also meant that they had to be clever. For example, they needed to work out the times of prayer, the direction of Makkah and how much tax to pay to charity. As a result, Muslims have made great contributions to education. Here are some examples:

- They have given the West Arabic numerals (1, 2, 3 etc.).
- Muslims were the first to use zero.
- They were the first to have a full system of decimals.
- Muslims invented algebra.
- They discovered many new stars.

Look at the words opposite. They are all Arabic words!

▲ *Just some of the Arabic words we still use today*

In the Middle Ages (about 1000–1400 CE), the Arab countries were more advanced than Western countries:

- In medicine, Muslim doctors were more skilled than Christian ones. They liked to use natural drugs and herbs, rather than surgery. They knew that a good diet and a healthy life-style were important for good health.
- Muslim traders travelled far overseas long before Western explorers like Columbus. Their maps were some of the finest of the time. Their earliest world maps show the Earth as round. Most Europeans still thought it was flat!
- People from all over Europe used the Muslim universities and libraries.

A special skill that Muslims have is weaving carpets, especially prayer mats. They have been making carpets for well over 1000 years. As Arabs, they have lived in tents with little furniture, but with beautiful rugs and cushions. But however beautiful the carpet, there is always a mistake. This carpet expert explains why:

> In any true Persian or Turkish rug, it should be possible to find the deliberate mistake. Muslims believe that only Allah makes things perfectly. I once knew a rug maker who believed this so much that it got him into trouble with his boss. Just before finishing each rug, he would make a deliberate mistake. Although he was afraid of his boss, he was even more afraid of offending Allah.
>
> Caroline Bosley: *Rugs to Riches*

1 Using the information on pages 61–62, draw an illustrated diagram to record at least FOUR things you use or know, which have come to us from Muslims.

2 Design a Muslim prayer mat.
- It should have an arch on it that can be pointed towards Makkah.
- It should not have any people or animals drawn on it.
- Decorate it with geometric patterns.
- Remember your deliberate mistake!

◀ *Muslims have been making prayer mats and carpets for over 1000 years*

Glossary

Allah – name for God in Islam
angel – messenger of God
Arabic – the language of the Arabs

Bismillah – first word of an Arabic phrase meaning 'In the name of God, the Merciful, the Compassionate'

calligraphy – beautiful writing
circumcised – the loose skin at the tip of the penis is cut off
compassionate – taking pity on
cremation – a dead body is burnt to ashes

fast – to go without food
Five Pillars – 5 duties of Muslims

Gabriel – the angel who is believed to have spoken to Muhammad

Hadith – record of what Muhammad said and did
hajj – the Great Pilgrimage to Makkah
hajja – a woman who has done the hajj
hajji – a man who has done the hajj
halal – allowed
haram – not allowed
Hijrah – Muhammad's move to Madinah

id – Arabic word for festival
idol – thing that is worshipped, such as a statue
Id-ul-Adha – the festival which comes at the end of pilgrimage
Id-ul-Fitr – the festival which comes at the end of fasting
imam – religious leader at a mosque

Islam – name of the Muslim religion

Ka'bah – cube-shaped building in Makkah
Khadijah – Muhammad's first wife

Makkah – the centre of Islam
mihrab – alcove in wall of mosque showing the direction of Makkah
minaret – tall tower for calling Muslims to prayer
minbar – raised platform for imam to preach from
mosque – Muslim place of worship
Muhammad – the Messenger of God, key figure in Islam
Muslim – a follower of Islam

pilgrimage – a religious journey to a holy place
prophet – someone who speaks for God
prostration – bowing down low

Ramadan – the month of fasting

sacrifice – to give up something for someone you love
Shahadah – declaration of faith, the first Pillar
Shi'ite – Muslims who belong to Ali's 'group'
Sunni – main Muslim group, they claim to follow the right 'path'

Qur'an – the holy book of Islam

zakah – tax given to charity

Index